I0420772

How Great Products Get Made

By Girish Lakshminarayana

To Ruhi

Section 1

Unlearn

What Design is

If I ask you what design is…

If you struggle to tell me what it is… or if you couldn't be bothered… that's a good sign.

I feel it's easier then, to digest this book.

Design is a loaded word.

Defining what design is is a very good starting point. The word design should no longer be used, I think. We need a new word.

The Starting Point

UX, Design Thinking, UI Design, Aesthetics

…are all a part of Design, the over-arching idea of Design.

Design has nothing to do with skills.

It starts with having experienced really good design at some point. Like good food, your interest in Sushi or Chinese food might start with that one amazing dish you had.

You need that one experience. It probably has to be a mind-blowing one as well.

Production starts with consumption. This is the beginning of the education of design.

How do I put this seed into you? I love these products:

Apple products

Workflowy.com

Hipmunk.com

Basecamp.com

These products evoke emotion. People don't just like them, they love them. They become fans. Thousands of them. Creating fans is probably the aim of design.

Oh, I also like the Mailbox App

Design is Probably How You Understand The Problem

It starts with the definition of the problem itself; All the assumptions that go into what the problem is.

It's important to not even give it a name that has too much meaning. Because names with meaning pre-suppose what the problem is. Or worse, what the solution should be.

It's worth our while many times spending time re-defining the problem statement itself.

Design Is The Missing Link

UX misses it. Programming misses the point.

Architecture misses the point. UI is definitely not the answer.

It's not even Design Thinking.

They are all a part of the spirit of design.

Steve Jobs said design is *giving a damn*.

It's probably true.

There is Also Emotional Design

My favorite dishes are not just edible, they are really tasty.

Software that just does the job is like edible food.

It need not be like that.

Emotional design reacts to the humanness in us.

Emotional connections with the user are born out of products that have a personality.

Personality = Emotion

If your product was a person, who would it be?

Who **all** would it be?

Design Consciously

The first huts by early humans were designed unconsciously.

The huts would work for a while but fail when the climate changed, or cholera spread because of accumulated filth. So they worked on it. They added a door. Then windows. They added this, they added that.

It was reactive. Trial and error. It was a really slow process.

Here we are talking about conscious design. All the design tools and methods we learn should only add to how consciously and predictively we design.

Design is conscious decision making.

Governments Are Unconscious

The worst products and services come out of government-run organizations. That's typical. They have very little competition many times.

They stop caring about their user. They start doing the opposite of good design.

Good design is caring.

Section 2

The Basics

Affordances

A chair needs no instruction manual. You know where everything goes and what to use it for.

Affordances are what a user can get away with.

Affordances are what a user can get away with doing to and with your product.

Sooner or later, they will put it to those uses.

We can design keeping this tendency in mind.

What signals **are** our products giving out about their use?

What signals **should** they be giving out?

What should they absolutely **not** give out?

My 3 year old daughter can get away with swiping for pictures on her IPad.

She also throws it to the floor sometimes.

Forces

There is a saying in design: *Form follows function*.

This makes sense.

A sand dune in the desert forms exactly the way it is supposed to form. It acknowledges all the forces acting on it.

It feels natural. It feels right.

A good product has this effect. It feels right. It feels obvious too.

It's also when design seems to disappear from the product. It acknowledges all the forces that act on it.

Continually.

This is a nice way of thinking about product design.

Technical constraints, budget limitations, user tendencies, technical savvy of the user etc. are the forces in this case.

Bombarding your customer with questions that reveal all possible constraints that product needs to work within is a good place to start.

That's your job.

This is also what they call Design Thinking.

More Scope = More Uncertainty

Not all forces need to be acknowledged by the product. We can group them and address the ones that we can easily handle at this time.

This is because scope makes things uncertain.

When you have certainty you are proud of the place you are at with your product. You tend to show it around a lot more. It tends to create a buzz and anticipation as well. Always be moving from a place you are proud of about your product.

This is an over-arching principle. The one that I always remember and abide by all the way through the lifecycle of product development.

Cutting features out ruthlessly is very much a part of the design process.

Because, scope IS uncertainty.

The 3rd Iteration

I have come to realize that new product development typically goes through these typical iterations.

1. The 1st iteration is about hustle, speed and getting things done fast.
2. The 2nd iteration is when the feedback and learnings gathered from the results of the 1st iteration are acted on.
3. The 3rd iteration is when you typically need to rework the architecture itself and all the open loops/bugs need to be closed.

These iterations create an illusion that we have something to judge at the end of each one. That's not the case.

We need to get to the 3rd iteration as quickly as possible.

Till then we don't actually have a product.

The Idea of "Jobs-to-be-done"

How do you sell more milk shakes?

First, let's understand what the job is that we are hiring the milk shake to do. Clayton Christenson talks about how he came to this realization while working for his client who manufactures milk shakes.

He discovered that the client's customers wanted something to do when they were on their morning commute driving into the city for work.

They needed something that would last the ride and also the other options wouldn't do the job all that well on the commute:

Coffee - too hot

Banana - finishes quickly

Doughnut - makes their fingers messy

Milk shakes did the job quite well.

To sell more, the answer was obvious. Make the milkshake thicker and crunchier so it could **last the ride** and also **fill them up** a little bit, all while **allowing them to drive** with **clean hands**. Those were the jobs the users were hiring the milk shake to do.

Similarly, I want to know the weather because I need to know if I should take an umbrella to work today. Weather services can directly instruct people what to wear.

"Who is your customer?" is no longer a relevant question.

The right question is: "What is the job that your users are hiring your product to do?"

The "Jobs-to-be-done" idea is probably the best insight that has come out in the last few decades that dramatically improves the design process.

The house you live in currently - What jobs do you need it to do for you?

What jobs does your house do for you?

Here are the main jobs my house needs to do:

1. To help me sleep comfortably
2. To get me out of the house to the office in the morning as quickly as possible
3. To feed me quickly and healthily
4. To help me relax
5. To entertain me, my family and friends when they come over
6. To provide my family security – especially when we are sleeping
7. To allow me to Work/read in peace and quiet

All the things you buy for your home and the way they are arranged can now be influenced by the jobs-to-be-done question.

How do you know you have a house that does its job?

Ask yourself if you sleep well there, work in peace and with concentration, does your house feel fun, intimate and relaxing? Does your family feel secure?

Optimize for each of the jobs above.

Design is a Continuous Process

Design is iterative. On an ongoing basis, here are the aspects that you will iterate on, almost daily :

You constantly add features that do more jobs for the user.

You acknowledge more forces.

You constantly simplify and prune features that don't work well.

You make the affordances a little better.

Your product gets shinier and more usable.

Bad design should feel more and more irritating to you.

2 types of thinking

We are now thinking about thinking. Convergent thinking and Divergent thinking.

We need divergent thinking when we are out of ideas. Actually, too much convergent thinking is why you run out of ideas.

We need to diverge especially at the beginning of a project.

To diverge is to blow up and have as many options as possible.

In the beginning of a project, you want to blow up all the wide range of options, consider taking risks, get creative, ideate, brainstorm, think big – to diverge is to blow up and have as many options as possible.

We go for sheer quantity of ideas rather than quality of ideas.

The idea for Twitter is born out of this sort of thinking.

Nothing crazy is ever born out of convergent thinking.

Convergence assumes a box to think inside of.

The problem with too much divergent thinking is that the options keep increasing and at some point start opposing each other.

The more you diverge, the more confused you get. The scope increases and so does the uncertainty.

If a project is "not getting off the ground" it's typically because of too much divergence and lack of convergent thinking.

Diverge only till you get a sense of closure. You feel satisfied with the number of options and then you stop. The thinking should now shift to convergent mode.

Be Merciless

Convergent thinking is in play in every aspect of your life.

> When you shop for clothes

> When you want to go for a movie

> When your family is deciding which restaurant to dine in

> When you are choosing a partner to get married to

To get things done, you diverge first and then converge onto one doable solution.

Somebody has to cut down on the options at some time.

There is mercilessness to convergence.

Be merciless.

When you are doing that, you are designing.

Design is a pulsating process

...between Divergence and Convergence. And both can happen many times over in any project.

A simple thing like a product name can block divergence. Be careful not to name your project with something meaningful especially in the beginning. A name presumes some solutions and blocks ideation.

So when do we stop diverging.

I stop diverging when I am satisfied that the ideas we have produced matches our ambitions: like "being the best" "being the easiest product in the market" etc

And when I stop converging there is a sense of calm and relief in the room.

A lack of divergence and too much convergence leads to unambitious products. It's boring.

Convergence almost always produces action. Convergent questions assume that action will follow. Example: "Let's vote for the movie we want to see from this list".

It's a sort of dictatorship.

Can you identify with these situations: Have you been in situations where there is much more of one sort of thinking than the other?

But now...

Knowing you will converge later on you can diverge as much as you want.

Knowing you have diverged enough means you can very sure of the option you have finally converged upon.

Diverge

Here are the verbs that help me diverge:

Enhance

Defer Judgement

Using the "Yes-and" technique

Playing with an idea

Visualize

Combine

Integrate

Fantasize

Go big

Go wide

Imagine ("What if" scenarios)

Look for the unusual

Increase

Explore

Converge

Here are the verbs that help me converge

Get clear

Decrease options

Pick something

Rate/vote all the options

Categorize

Refine

Decide

Contract

Hone in

Focus

Reduce

Discern

Cluster

Section 3

The Design Mindset

A Way of Working

When I was in college, I was determined to read all the text books, end to end, multiple times. I would make enormous plans and draw schedules to help me execute it.

But it would never happen.

When the time for the examinations came, I would study 80% of my stuff on the day before the examination. Somehow my mind had prioritized which portions of the text I needed to study and would converge on actually studying it.

I would always be amazed at how much got done at the last minute. I would always be left with the thought that if I had studied even a week before the examination "in this mode", I would have fared 5 times better in the examination.

Today, I apply this to product development.

Let's do an experiment.

Think of a project that you are working on currently.

Think of the current "to-do" list for the project. What's undone? How long will each of the items take?

As you are thinking about it, what if I told you that you have only 30 minutes left to work on that project? For All Time! You will never get to work on it again, ever.

What finishing touches will you provide in 30 minutes? Think of all the 5 minute activities you can do to give it some sort of closure. What else can you cram into the 30 minute window?

At the end of 30 minutes, I won't take it away from you of course and you have an additional 30 minutes. What else can you do now?

Can you keep this state through the project?

Did you see how the thinking shifted to finiteness? How it was suddenly manageable and practical? And converged?

Nothing gets work done like the last-minute.

What if we could have multiple last-minutes?

We will achieve a sense of closure and provide a polish to the product that was never there before.

Achieving Noticeability

Instead of constantly working on making the product better, what if you also work on making it slightly different?

Even just 1percent different.

Seth Godin talks about the purple cow effect. If you saw a purple cow on the way to work, you would probably talk about it with your co-workers even though you saw hundreds of normal colored cows as well.

Our minds notice anything that breaks a pattern.

Can we make our products 1% different?

We can go in this direction as makers.

The Biggest Advantage

Products that decide to do only one thing have a huge strategic advantage:

1. It forces you to get really good at it
2. You will likely be proud of your product and it shows
3. It comes built in with an easy heuristic to measure success or failure
4. Customers also tend to appreciate your dedication and give you a special place in their minds and associate you with that one thing
5. For the customers, it's easy to give definite feedback on the product since it does just one thing

Eliminate Misunderstandings

Look for the potential to misunderstand your product.

Force yourself to find 10 ways people can misunderstand, misinterpret, get confused by your product's interface and micro copy.

Just this one activity can dramatically improve a product.

This is caring pro-actively.

If Your Product Was A Service

Ideally, using your product should feel like a service provided by a human expert.

That's how good a product can potentially get.

In fact, it's a good idea to manually do what your product does to see how you would approach the situation. You can then bring the elements of humanness into the actual product.

A Word on Visual Design

User Interface design is also a part of Design.

UI is about aesthetics. The field of UI design studies what attracts or repels us.

It's also a study of our reptilian and mammalian brains.

This is also what makes design complicated. Not only does the product have to be intelligent, it has to appeal to our emotions (governed by our mammalian brain) and baser instincts like fight or flight response (governed by our reptilian brain)

UI design is a massive field and is not the scope of this book.

There is a phrase for the UI design principles: "The Universal Principles of Design".

Getting a basic understanding of the universal principles is of great value.

The universal principles of design are a set of guidelines for things like:

Symmetry

Typography

Hierarchy

Alignment

Visual Organization

Color theory

These are the basics. Knowing them really helps in understanding our animal brain.

I got everything I wanted to know from a book called "The Universal Principles of Design" by William Lidwell.

I would highly recommend buying and using the book as a constant reference manual.

How Long To Expertise

We like things that make us feel like an expert.

Will your product make me feel like one?

Will I feel like an expert of your product the first time I use it?

My little 3 year old is an expert on the IPad.

Or does it require me to build my expertise with effort and training.

Some products require you to be an employee of the makers company to get anywhere near using it. That's a bad product

Design Is Dictatorship

Not for the users.

Internally, for the company it is.

This is because of how the brain works.

It's hard to combine our aesthetics. It's hard for 2 mammalian/reptilian brains to agree on one aesthetic.

Design that comes from some strong opinions can be fanatically appealing to some and revolting to the other.

This is ok.

All the Apple products are white. Someone there is dictating terms.

Design Is A Conscious Set Of Decisions Made About The Product

There should be at least 2 reasons for every design decision.

Why?

Because, it makes for a more conscious design.

Every aspect of the product can be questioned this way.

This forces you to second guess and predict what could go wrong.

In product team meetings, this could also be a way of prioritizing which features should be built first.

Section 4

Forms of Design

Emotional Design

I know people who give their bikes names. They seem to have an emotional connection with their bikes and the brand of the bike.

Emotion for the product can be engineered.

To create emotion your product needs to have a personality.

What's an appropriate personality for your product?

You want it to be serious? Who is the most serious person you know then?

You can add elements of this person into the product.

This can dictate the tone of the product, the words used in communication and even the interface of the product.

Your product can also be a mix of multiple personalities.

Also, consider the user's feelings as they go through the different stages of using your product.

What the toughest spots for the user? When are they uncertain, confused, annoyed etc?

How can you make those parts better for them? How would you lead them through it if you were physically there with them? It's helpful to map out the emotional journey of the user.

Addressing emotions like this takes your product to a different level. It changes how your users feel about your product, how they remember it, the image they give it and also how they talk about the product to other people.

Apple, Mailchimp and Slack do this beautifully.

Steve jobs' comment that Design is simply "giving a damn" – makes a lot of sense suddenly.

Make it fun

You don't have to add fun features into your app.

Just add the fun into existing features.

The opposite of fun

The opposite of this is to ask yourself, "what's the most engineering-heavy part of my product"

It's likely the least fun part of the product as well.

If there is too much engineering, a little bit of emotion and fun can help.

Things that just work

Do I have to make your product work? Or does it work anyway?

Many government products work if I make it work. I have to read pages and pages of confusing documentation, fill in all the forms and wait and follow up multiple times and yeah, it might just work.

One of the main objectives of the UX professional is to get the product to the stage that it works anyway, even in the face of mistakes by the user.

Pushing the envelop

When I run out of ideas, I ask myself this question.

On a scale of 1 to 10 where would you rate your product?

Let's suppose you give it a 7.

I will make it 4.

Now, how do get it back to 7? What would you do?

This could trigger some divergent thinking

Teach grandma over the phone

...or at least in person.

This is a good test of your understanding of the product.

If you cannot do this, it's possible your product is too complicated.

It will also tell you all the assumptions you are making about the user's skill level.

The 'AHA' moment

Let's compare your product to Sushi food. Because, that's how alien it is to new users.

For most people it takes a few tries before they like Sushi.

Many "get it" after a few tries.

It hits a spot.

How long does your product take to hit the spot?

We can call this the "Aha moment" in the product usage timeline. Many times, the "aha moment" is the same spot in the usage timeline for a large section of the users. They all seem to "get it" at the same moment.

For Twitter, it was after the new users followed 25 people. Once they followed 25 people, they never seemed to look back. They get the whole point of why twitter exists in the first place and how it can help them as well. That's the tipping point. Now, their current signup flow is optimized to help get users to follow 20 people.

Our job is then to get all our first time users to their 'Aha moment' as soon as possible. Not just the tech savvy ones.

Onboarding – is another word to describe this. It's job is to answer the question "What's the point of you?"

Everything the users sees, reads, experiences and does during the onboarding process should add to their understanding about what the product is leading to the final 'aha moment'

It's a pity if you lose the users before that.

It means the design has failed.

Section 5

Everyday Design

I am stuck in my shoes

This is the biggest problem in design – that I am in MY shoes all the time. "I" am the problem.

I hope you are seeing that pattern.

It seems to me that every time I am able to step into the shoes of my users, I am designing.

Almost all the good tools, techniques and processes seem to help us step out of my shoes and into the user's.

I then slip back. I love it there - back in my shoes.

When I am in my shoes, my ability to give a damn goes to zero.

Knowing this tendency of mine, can I step out of it at least once a day and become the user for a second?

Here is one more way of stepping into their shoes

Expertise works against you

If you had zero skills to do the job of producing the product you are producing, what would the product look/work like?

What if a plumber designed it?

Or a stand-up comedian?

Copywriting is design

Words are very important.

Here are some questions you can ask about your copy:

Exactly how many seconds does the user need to understand what the product is?

How could this text confuse the users?

How does the user feel at this moment?

Is this memorable?

Why this order/arrangement?

What does this teach them?

Can I simplify this? Can this be clearer?

What are the assumptions made here?

What will happen next?

What just happened?

What's the problem?

What's the benefit/relief?

To Simplify

Remove – All things complicated, unnecessary, unused, fancy, redundant, things built out of insecurity, things that don't work

Hide – All advanced stuff, things that are used less than 20% of the time by people who know the product well.

Organize – All the things that belong together, things that come in a particular order, things that are used more vs things that are used less, things that feel cluttered

Displace – All the things that belong to a different context. Example: Displace complicated settings options from the Remote Control to the DVD player.

Design your design process

A lot of good design is about iteration. Nobody gets it right in the first iteration itself.

So set yourself up for iterative development. Try and get into a situation where iteration is natural and inevitable.

Which means that feedback on your product should be quick and frequent.

This naturally happens if you are one of the users of the product.

If not, learn the user's world by living in it and feeling their pain in your body.

It helps to just fake it and use the product like they would use it every day. Use it all the time pretending to be the user.

Then you are solving problems at a visceral level. Then you can truly say to your users - 'I feel your pain'

Another method is to simply hire industry experts to test and give you ready feedback.

Good design is iterative.

Give everything scale by allocating resources

Let's say you have identified certain design priorities.

This could be a feature that is key to the product.

It is your make-or-break feature.

You want to make sure it is the best it can be.

So we allocate a person or team to exclusively work on it. Hold meetings to discuss just this one feature. Even reserve a room for it. Throw money at it if needed. Track and measure its progress every day.

That was you are allowing it to scale – because you allocated resources, it will scale.

Google does this with its search, doesn't it? There is an obvious focus on the Google search functionality. They even measure their speed. This is the core. So they treat it as such.

This could also be for an aspect of the product like "speed" or "UX" or "Personality" – allocate resources and it tends to achieve scale.

Large companies talk a lot about innovation in their internal newsletters, but many do not even allocate 5% of employee time to R&D. Pure intent is nothing. Things take shape and scale because someone put money/time/effort where their mouth is.

Don't fix all the problems at once

This especially happens on the second iteration of product development which I consider the most dangerous iteration of all. It's called the Second System Effect.

Beware of the Second System Effect. It's killed a lot of potentially good products.

The first iteration has a certain innocence and speed to it.

Then you have learnt too much about what's wrong with the product the second time around.

The tendency then is to go at it with all the might and solve all the 140 things that are wrong with it.

But, scope = uncertainty

So more often than not, the project fails.

It's important to pick and batch the problems we will fix this time around.

Justify/Curate

There should be at least 2 reasons for a feature being a part of your product.

Go for the feature that converges multiple ideas.

That's always something magical about such a feature.

Curation, not accumulation is the goal of product development. Your product should **curate** some of the best features available in the market, not accumulate ALL of them.

This is where theming becomes very important. Curation happens around a theme.

In the beginning, while you are diverging, look for what the theme of the product should be. That will dictate what features "fit" and which ones are obvious misfits.

Constraints are interesting

Curation, not accumulation is the goal of product development.

So your product should be interesting for what it doesn't do.

Twitter comes to mind. It doesn't allow more than 140 characters. Otherwise, it's just a blog.

Twitter doesn't allow blogging.

Section 6

Snake Oil

.

What about Virality?

Is there any use at all talking about virality or is it like predicting the weather?

Let's find out what it is and I will let you make the judgement.

If an existing user of your product brings in one other user to use your product and a little bit more, then your product is viral.

Let me say that again.

If every user of your product, on average, recommends and brings in just a little bit more than 1 user to come and use your product, your product can be called viral.

In fact, you can't help but have a viral product. Because the marketing costs to acquire the additional users falls to zero.

Let's say a thousand users have purchased this book so far.

If all of you recommend it to your friends and more than one of your friends end up purchasing my book, then this book will go viral. It will spread exponentially and on its own.

I didn't have to market it to the additional users. You did.

And all your friends, as a rule, should end up getting one or 2 of **their** friends to read this book and so on...

This can go out of control very quickly. It's called exponential growth. It's anybody's favorite form of growth.

Exponential growth is unstoppable.

Like a nuclear reaction.

A Long time ago an Indian king had the habit of challenging wise visitors to a game of chess.

One day a traveling sage was challenged by the king and offered any reward he wanted.

The sage modestly asked just for a few grains of rice in the following manner: The king was to put a single grain of rice on the first chess square and double it on every consequent one till the 64th square.

Of course, the king played and lost the game.

He then ordered a bag of rice to be brought to the chess board.

While placing rice grains according to the arrangement: 1 grain on the first square, 2 on the second, 4 on the third, 8 on the fourth and so on, he realized that the amount of rice required would be the equivalent of covering the surface area of the earth twice, oceans included.

Imagine if there was one more square on the chess board!

In other words, this is what happened to Facebook. They grew exponentially.

The king didn't understand exponential growth.

Exponential growth is surprisingly deceptive. Look at an imagined scenario where Facebook is growing exponentially month on month. What would the user base look like a month before they hit a billion users?

It would have Just 500 million users.

And just a 6 months before that? Just 6 million users.

Nobody would have known. Exponential growth is like a runaway train.

It's a very useful thing to happen.

Apps like Twitter, Facebook and Dropbox HAD to have grown exponentially. There is just no way they would have reached that many people by growing linearly.

Word of mouth plays a huge role in exponential growth.

It's also prevalent much more in B2C companies and not so much in B2B companies.

B2B companies typically ask for money. Asking for money inhibits exponential growth.

The other quality viral products tend to have is that they are useless when used by just one person.

Email, Paypal, Facebook and Twitter are useless when you use it alone.

If I want to receive money in Paypal, someone should be there to send it.

Facebook's value to the user increases as the number of people/friends on it increases.

So the user comes back for more. It's a virtuous, self-propagating cycle.

Football is viral

It's no surprise to me that Football is the most popular game on the planet.

Let's look at some of its properties.

It is played on a massive field so a lot of people can watch it being played.

It has almost no learning curve, the ball has to be kicked into the net, everyone gets that the first time they see the game being played.

And all you need is a ball to start playing it.

It requires you to have 2 teams to play so more people get recruited naturally to the game.

It only takes about 30 minutes to get a meaningful result.

Compare that to Chess.

The playing area is not visible to maybe more than 3 or 4 people around the chess board.

It has a very steep learning curve.

You only need 2 people to play chess.

It needs a chess board which is not always handy.

It's easy to see why football got popular.

It's safe to say that chess is never going to be the most popular game in the world.

Visibility helps Virality

All apple products are white. So if someone in a coffee shop is using any electronic device that's white people assume it's an Apple product.

When the original iPods came out, you could see who was using it with the distinct white ear phones.

The Apple product advertises itself. Visibility of use, as we have seen with the football example, helps in virality.

Social one-upmanship helps with Virality

If a product is exclusive, prestigious or is a major secret, people tend to talk about it more.

Gmail, when it first came in, needed an invite before you could sign up. It created exclusivity, curiosity and demand that really helped it grow into almost universal adoption.

A fast viral cycle helps virality

We know that something goes viral when existing users bring in at least one friend to a product.

It turns out that if an existing user brings in a friend to your product **next month**, it's not as useful as, if they were to bring a friend **today** or **right now**.

This is called the viral cycle.

It needs to be as fast as possible.

It also turns out that reducing the viral cycle is more valuable than increasing the number of friends brought in.

Let me say that again.

It turns out that reducing the **time taken** for the viral cycle to complete is more valuable than increasing the **ways** or the **number** of users a single friend brings into your application.

That way you multiply faster.

So it is helpful to make the viral cycle consciously faster.

Using social media to spread the word, reminding the user to spread the word, sometimes even bribing them are ways in which the viral cycle can be sped up.

The Viral Co-efficient

The Viral Co-efficient is a number. For most apps this value will be less than 1.

For truly viral apps this value will be greater than 1.

Which means that more than 1 person is brought in free by word of mouth for every user on the platform.

It helps to consciously increase this number.

The Viral Co-efficient need not always end up greater than 1.

A decent viral co-efficient can combine with traditional marketing channels to great effect.

So make sure all your users invite more than one person onto your app, somehow.

Dropbox did this. They gave away 250mb of free space to every friend I "converted" plus my friends who signed up through me got an additional 250mb above the normal storage. I ended up with 8 GB of free space because I made sure a lot of my friends signed up! Their default storage was just 2 GB. They bribed me to get them more users.

Here is a bunch of ways in which you can increase the viral co-efficient of your product.

How many people can you get your existing users to invite?

How can you make this process (of your users inviting their friends) easy for them?

Why would they invite?

Can you give them a real benefit?

How convincing is the invite?

Can you give their friend a benefit?

How quickly does the user invite another friend after he/she has signed up? Can we speed this up?

How quickly does the friend accept it?

How often does the user invite other people? Can we make it more frequent?

Multiple Loops

You can have multiple viral loops in your app.

In each viral loop, there could be a unique reason for the word-of-mouth.

One viral loop could be a straight forward bribe like Dropbox – get more space by inviting more people.

Another could be a "create a team" option.

This is actually quite popular. Here is user gets to create a team around his colleagues so they can off-load work, assign tasks and maybe get group discounts.

You can have both these in your product or more.

A word of caution here.

Virality without engagement is a shallow shell. You might grow very fast but people won't come back to your product and soon it will all collapse without an engaging product.

There are many apps which achieved Virality but fell flat after a period of tremendous growth.

Interestingly, products like this sometimes end up being indistinguishable from spam.

The Branchout app for Facebook comes to mind.

Habit Formation

The product has to become a part of your user's daily/weekly routine.

Unless that happens, you will still be obscure, even if you have a lot of "sing ups"

It's like signing up for the Gymnasium and never coming back after the first visit. They are not really a customer for the Gymnasium.

Sign-ups mean nothing. Growth by sign-ups means nothing unless it is engaging and becomes a habit.

Earlier we had discussed the Onboarding process as a concept.

Onboarding truly is not done until the product ends up being a habit.

This *ongoing onboarding* could last days and even weeks till after the sign-up date.

Facebook is a great example. It is tremendously successful not because of the number of users but because of the number of people who use it every day. It has 1.5 billion registered users and 968 daily users!

Engagement is a bigger secret of success than plain growth.

How do we engage the user?

Engagement is all in the mind. Engaging products eventually become a habit.

Habit formation is brilliant explored in "Hooked – How to build habit forming products" by Nir Eyal.

It all starts with **Triggers.** Your product needs to have triggers.

These could be internal or external. The views for the song Friday by Rebecca Black apparently shot up during Fridays. This is an example of an internal trigger. People started playing it as a joke and sending it to their friends come Friday.

External triggers could be emails, mobile text messages, mobile app notifications etc.

Amazon uses the "People who bought this also bought" section as a trigger to get people to click and see other products.

Triggers lead to **Actions**

Ideally the actions have to be very small and simple. Like a click. Taking the Amazon example above, the user is triggered to look at other products they could buy on Amazon. Then they click and read the article.

Actions are where the whole field of UX sits in, according to Nir, and should make the process friction free and intuitive.

Actions should lead to a **Variable reward**

The **Variable** part is extremely important. Rewards are great, but if the user can predict the reward, they will soon lose interest.

If they don't know what the reward is going to be, it increases the interest level tremendously.

This is to say that the anticipation of the reward is more exciting for the user than the reward itself.

An user tags you on Facebook and Facebook sends you an email notification (**Trigger**), you login to Facebook (**Action**) and are rewarded by the photograph of you at a party with your friend (**Reward**) plus all the other updates by your other friends (**Variable rewards**)

Which leads the user to **Investment**

Investment is the end game, the holy grail of habit formation. Without this, the earlier steps become meaningless.

Here we are talking about Investment by the user in your product.

Investment in the product could be things like adding more friends, or updating their profile.

Investment by the user should improve the experience of the product for them. So it's a good thing. The more friends I have on Facebook the more up to date I can stay with my friend's circle. The more complete my profile is on Linkedin, the more business opportunities might come my way.

Investments also setup the **Trigger – Action – Variable reward – Investment** cycle to happen again.

Once I **invest** by adding 10 new friends, the chances of a **trigger** happening (them tagging me) goes up and so does the **variable reward** (more status updates).

It sets up a virtuous cycle.

It should reach a point where it takes more effort to stop the cycle than to keep it going for the user. It's should take will power to **stop** using the product than to **let** the habit of using your product be.

That's when your product has become a habit.

www.ingramcontent.com/pod-product-compliance
Lightning Source LLC
Chambersburg PA
CBHW071237280526
45787CB00002B/964